ACE YOUR ACTING AUDITION

Published 2009 by S.O.M.E. Productions, New York, NY.

Website address: www.castingsolutions.tv

ISBN- 13: 978-0-9823462-0-4
ISBN- 10: 0-9823462-0-4

ACE YOUR ACTING AUDITION

Using Iconic Specificity™
and Other Surefire Techniques

By Liz Ortiz-Mackes

"Through Liz's career counseling sessions, and now this book, our acting students are able to begin their careers in a very positive manner. Liz always tells it like it is. Her efforts give students the confidence to pursue a professional career without fear and with high standards for themselves and their craft.

Thank you, Liz!"

-CONSTANTINE SCOPAS
Director of Instruction,
American Academy of Dramatic Arts, New York

CONTENTS

ACKNOWLEDGEMENTS 1

INTRODUCTION 2-3

CHAPTER 1: YOU ARE THE C.E.O. OF YOU 5-12

CHAPTER 2: AUDITION SABOTAGE – WHAT NOT
TO DO 13-20

CHAPTER 3: PREPARATION EQUALS LIBERATION 21-26

CHAPTER 4: THE TEXT IS YOUR FRIEND 27-30

CHAPTER 5: ICONIC SPECIFICITY™ 31-34

CHAPTER 6: THE MOMENT BEFORE AND THE MOMENT
AFTER - PUTTING YOUR AUDITION
IN A FRAME.. 35-38

CHAPTER 7: "NICE" EQUALS "NEXT" – MAKING YOUR
SECOND TAKE YOUR FIRST 39-44

CHAPTER 8: THE 3 P's: PROFESSIONALISM,
PRESENTATION & PROTOCOL 45-50

CHAPTER 9: SOMETIMES EAST IS WEST AND LESS IS MORE
– PLAYING THE UNEXPECTED 51-54

CHAPTER 10: THE COPY AS PROP – YOUR SECURITY
BLANKET AND OTHER GREAT USES 55-58

CHAPTER 11: YOU ARE WHAT YOU WEAR 59-64

CHAPTER 12: NOBODY WANTS TO WORK WITH
CRAZY.. 65-68

CHAPTER 13: WHAT'S MY STORY? 69-74

CHAPTER 14: IMPROVISATION - LOOKS EASY, BUT
IT'S NOT 75-78

CHAPTER 15: THEATRE = 10, FILM = 5: WALKING THE
BOARDS vs PLAYING TO THE LENS........ 79-84

CHAPTER 16: IT'S NOW OR NEVER - BEING "IN THE
MOMENT" AND STAYING THERE 85-88

CHAPTER 17: WHY YOU WON'T GET THE JOB – THE
CASTING MAZE IS A MINEFIELD 89-94

CHAPTER 18: MARKETING 101 - KNOW THYSELF 95-98

CHAPTER 19: FAITH OR FEAR – WHICH DO YOU BRING
WHEN YOU WALK INTO
THE ROOM? 99-104

TO ACTORS WITH DISABILITIES 105-106

ABOUT THE AUTHOR 107

RESOURCES 108

NOTES 109-110

ACKNOWLEDGEMENTS

Deepest thanks to : My completely accepting husband Steve for his love and editing skills. My three children Faith, Cole and Jeremiah; without them I am lost. My beloved Mother, Helen Ortiz for raising me in New York City. My dear friend Franz Reynold of the Screen Actors Guild Foundation, who witnessed my workshops dozens of times, encouraged me to write this book and believed that I could do it. My close friend and casting associate Cahill Connolly for designing this book beautifully. Your talent, unconditional loyalty, and support is the glue, that holds it all together. And finally, all the actors and acting students I've worked with over the years; you have taught me much; I dedicate this book to you.

-July, 2009, New York, NY

INTRODUCTION

There is a method to the madness called auditioning, but there are still many brilliant actors who have yet to master the fundamentals of this "necessary evil." Honest casting directors – like the author of this book – will admit that it's an often brutal experience for all involved, but unless you're producing your own projects (hint!), it will constitute a major part of your artistic endeavors.

I have observed first-hand the positive effect that Liz's no-frills acting pointers have had on hundreds of performers. The power lies in their simplicity, the succinct manner in which she has been able to distill the information from a flood of different acting styles into a few relevant nuggets that create the light bulb moment!

All too often, the performer is so pre-occupied with what "they" (the folks sitting behind the table) want that they sabotage their prospects with over-analysis. What the casting director wants – besides being able to wrap the session ASAP! – is for the actor to present the very best audition possible. In other words, they want to see your "A" game. What they get most of the time is a tame (read safe), uninspired interpretation of the text, coupled with ridiculous vocal levels, and inappropriate and unnecessary "business." This is the sort of presentation that screams "amateur" and instantly eliminates the actor from the callback sweepstakes.

A successful audition requires a combination of focus and vision – the ability to eliminate everything but what's absolutely essential in that moment, to deliver the best performance of the material at hand. And it helps immensely if the actor has a bold vision of who and what the character is so that they can convincingly transform themselves into a fully realized persona. That's the kind of performance that will always leave a very favorable impression!

Timing, tenacity, and talent are all essential elements to creating success as a performer. That and the right attitude will place you on the path to a rewarding career. Leave the bad childhood and the tortured existence outside the audition session. Demonstrating emotional imbalance of any sort will instantly land you in the reject bin, and rightly so. No one should have to put up with the stupidity and self-centered unraveling of some deluded being with an artistic bent – life is too short!

When all is said and done, it doesn't much matter how many years of training as an actor you have had, even if you've been fortunate to attend the very best schools. The truth is, if in the crunch, you are unable to deliver a knockout audition, then you'll be damned to working background for the rest of your life.

The great information contained in this book just might save you from that fate!

– FRANZ REYNOLD
Screen Actors Guild Foundation

CHAPTER 1

YOU ARE THE C.E.O. OF YOU

Imagine your acting career as a series of interconnected links forming an endless chain of possibilities. You are the first link, and, as the old saying goes, "you're only as strong as your weakest link." Begin by accepting that you are the C.E.O. of "Y.O.U.", the Chair Person of "ME Incorporated." This is a decision you should make when you decide to become a member of the professional acting community. After witnessing countless auditions over the years, the common trait shared by actors who booked the job or came close, is an energetic projection of connectivity, confidence and radiance. What I just described is invisible. It's not a tool you can download. It springs from taking responsibility and choosing to control your own destiny. This choice fundamentally falls into three categories: Mindset, Lifestyle and Physicality.

MINDSET

Your mindset is the foundation of your audition or interview. Like concrete being poured into the base of a home, your mindset is what supports everything else. Identify your feelings about yourself first and every aspect of the upcoming audition, interview or meeting. Keeping a journal is an invaluable tool for self-exploration and knowledge. By having a private, safe place to chart your feelings, ideas, inspirations, experiences etc., you are acknowledging your mindset.

Creating a Mindset Worksheet is a quick way to check on yourself.

Mindset Worksheet

Today's date:

Today I feel:

Date of audition/interview/meeting:

I will be meeting:

Purpose of audition/interview/meeting:

Thinking about this audition/interview/meeting, makes me feel:

When I go in, I'd like to feel:

Actions I can do to improve my mindset:

Going for the comfortable and familiar are two of the quickest ways to improve and boost a mindset.

The following is an example of a completed Mindset Worksheet. Using this exercise can prove invaluable in identifying your mindset and guiding yourself proactively.

Today's date: *2-19-09*

Today I feel: *tired and stressed*

Date of audition/interview/meeting: *2-21-09*

I will be meeting: *Jane Doe, Casting Director for ABC Theatre Company*

Purpose of audition/interview/meeting: *audition for Glass Menagerie, role of LAURA*

Thinking about this audition/interview/meeting right now, makes me feel: *nervous and insecure, I don't know if I have what it takes for such a dream role*

When I go in, I'd like to feel: *like a fresh new LAURA, delivering an inspiring, killer audition*

Actions I can do to improve my mindset: *read script, "Google" the people I'm meeting, workout, rent the DVD*

By describing the upcoming audition/interview/meeting and listing your feelings about it, you are able to manage the unavoidable stress or insecurity. Acknowledging how you feel is a powerful first step in your audition preparation.

LIFESTYLE

You have identified your mindset regarding how you feel about your place in the industry and the experiences within it. The second component to claiming your membership in the professional acting community is lifestyle. A lifestyle is the all-encompassing expression of every detail and action that informs your day-to-day existence. These parts will consciously move you closer toward your professional acting goals as you become synergistically charged about them. When you feel weighed down by life's responsibilities and obligations, i.e. the survival job, rent, food, classes, etc., your sense of being becomes fragmented, allowing frustration or bitterness to cloud the scene.

It all comes down to how you choose to perceive where your life is or should be at this exact moment.

"My survival job is boring."

"I never have enough money to pay rent and bills."

"I'm too depressed to audition properly."

"Why haven't I made it yet?"

TO MAKE MORE EMPOWERED CHOICES, ALL YOU HAVE TO DO IS "FLIP THE SCRIPT." YOU MUST COME TO ACCEPT THAT DESPITE THESE "OBSTACLES" YOU CAN FIND THE STRENGTH TO OVERPOWER THEM AND CREATE A SUCCESSFUL CAREER.

Productive Perceptions and Choices

"My survival job means I won't be a starving artist."

"I will work out a payment plan with my creditors."

"Each day, I will find at least one opportunity to audition or work on my craft."

"It doesn't matter when I make it, as long as I remain passionate about being an artist."

PHYSICALITY

You have the mindset, and you've decided to live the lifestyle; now it's time to incorporate your physicality into a package that can only be defined by you. A corporate logo is associated with a product, i.e.

the golden arches represent McDonald's globally. Likewise, how you package your physical and energetic aspects will help you create a "brand" that is highly marketable. Creating your brand starts with paying attention to detail and playing up your unique aspects. Ask yourself: What would the logo of "ME Incorporated" look like?

Creating an Image Check List can help in identifying and refining the "brand" that is you.

Image Check List

My three strongest physical characteristics are:

My three best personality traits are:

The type of clothing that is most flattering on me is:

The colors that look best on me are:

My hair stylist/barber suggests my hair looks best when:

I can improve my skin care routine by:

The makeup/grooming products I currently use are:

Makeup/grooming products I would like to try are:

By doing a quick self-inventory and getting feedback from trusted friends or experts, you can devise a specific direction on how to best present yourself to the industry. Don't underestimate how relevant your looks and feelings are in forming the first impression you make on others. If your physicality demonstrates that you are well-groomed, comfortable with yourself and prepared for that audition/interview/meeting before speaking a word, then you are ahead of the game.

AUDITION HOT TIP #1

When you are auditioning for a specific role, apply the Image Check List to the character you're preparing. Small details make a huge difference; don't overlook them.

CHAPTER 2

AUDITION SABOTAGE – WHAT NOT TO DO

"To sabotage or not to sabotage, that is the question."

My experience as a casting director leads me to believe that a great many actors are afflicted by a debilitating condition. They are suffering from a silent career killer: subconscious self –sabotage. It strikes at the most inopportune moments, in various forms, undermining their audition.

The following is a list of common audition mistakes actors make, which have nothing to do with acting.

1. Bring Your Damn Headshot and Resume to the Audition

This is a major pet peeve of mine. My clients like to hold and look at the actor's picture and resume and expect to be presented with their own set of potential candidates for the roles being cast when the auditions are done. No matter how digital or "green" things are these days, many industry professionals still like to stimulate their tactile senses with hardcopies of the actors headshots. Excuses for falling short in this regard ("I thought my agent sent it.") will mark you as unprofessional. And if my client who is either a director, producer, ad-executive, etc. wants a copy of your picture and resume then they should have that option readily available. It is your responsibility as a professional actor to always have your picture and resume on you, just about everywhere you go, in case it is needed. Remember, your headshot is your calling card; don't leave home without it.

2. Be On Time

Poor time management is poor self-management. It sends the message that you have little regard for the people who called you in to audition. Excluding emergencies, be realistic when planning your day. If you allocate, say, only thirty minutes during your lunch break from your "day job" to travel to and from your audition, and also actually audition, you'll never make it unless you know how to travel at warp speed. From the time you arrive at an audition location, allow yourself at least a half-hour for a commercial or industrial audition and forty-five minutes for legit (film, TV, theatre). You may be in and out of the session quickly or, as is often the case, it may take a bit longer than expected. Arriving late makes a negative impression before you even enter the room. Take responsibility for the controllable aspects of your audition preparation, your schedule being chief among them.

3. Know Where You're Going

When you arrive at your audition, look for a sign or ask where the sign-in/waiting area is for the specific casting session. Usually there will be a table with a sign-in sheet and possibly other paperwork pertaining to the project being cast. If you are waiting in the wrong place and don't sign in, the casting director won't know if you have arrived or not. Sign in within fifteen minutes of your appointment and only when you feel ready to be called in. If you have arrived early enough and need time to center yourself, do that first and then sign in.

4. Know Your Schedule

Casting is always contingent upon a production schedule. It is an absolute act of self-sabotage if you lead the casting director, producers, etc. to believe you are available and all of a sudden, you're not. This, of course, excludes unexpected emergencies. Most projects will have a general idea when they will start shooting or begin rehearsals. Be upfront about your potential schedule conflicts only if they cannot be changed. If you really want the role, and you're willing to quit your day job and move mountains, then you technically don't have any schedule conflicts. However, if you are on hold for another acting job or have other unshakeable commitments, you absolutely need to inform the casting director. Being honest from the start is to your advantage. If you are ideal for a role, the producers, director, etc. may be willing to work around your schedule.

5. Know Who and What You're Auditioning For

Ideally, you should be confident and prepared when you walk into an audition. To reach that state, learn everything you can about the specific project, role and the people involved. Search engines like Google and IMDB, among countless others, make this task relatively simple. Enter every name, title and venue, and then start researching. If you are auditioning for a commercial, research the product and the advertising agency; if it's a play, research the playwright and the theatre company; then read the play. The more you familiarize yourself with the project, the more your subconscious will become comfortable with the idea of auditioning. If you are auditioning for a film or TV project, ask the casting office if a copy of the entire script is available for you to read.

If you are auditioning for a commercial, ask if the copy is available in advance. Research as much as you can about the product, the corporation who manufactures it and the product's features. In many cases, commercial copy is not available until you arrive for the audition. If that is the case, get to the casting session early and ask for the copy immediately. Being armed with as much prior knowledge as possible helps project an aura of authentic self-assurance during your audition.

6. "In My Own Little Corner, in My Own Little World..."

Preparation, confidence, intelligence, positive energy and enthusiasm are key elements to a successful audition. The quickest way to diminish that energy and hard work is to give it away in the waiting area. I've found, over the years that many actors who regularly get callbacks and book the job share the trait of creating a private space for themselves while they are waiting to be called in. An audition is not a social event. Take advantage of your waiting time to focus and center yourself. You're not being rude to your fellow actors, you are prioritizing what's important to you. A good way to relax and connect to yourself while waiting is to listen (using headphones) to music associated with the role for which you are auditioning. For instance, if your audition is for a film that takes place in the late 1970's, then listen to music from that era. This will creatively place you in the setting of the script. If you are unable to find specific music that correlates to a role, jazz improvisation is a great stand-by option. Miles Davis was a master at this technique, where each note, like every word a character speaks, is expressed as a spontaneous surprise, a gift to be cherished. Jazz improvisation, as inspiration and preparation for an audition, works brilliantly because the music is rooted in artistry, discipline and technique. Containing yourself in this way is a far more empowering choice than losing focus because you were gossiping with your competition in the waiting area.

7. Keep it to Yourself, Less is More

You can't predict how your audition will go or what the mood of the room will be like when you go in. Understandably, you will have nervous energy. Recognize this for what it is: an indication that you care about the audition. Instead of resisting that energy, embrace it as a way to proactively fuel yourself. When you walk in, simply say, "Hi, thanks for seeing me." Place any personal belongings beside the door to both prevent leaving anything behind and to ensure a smooth exit. If the casting director, director or producer etc. asks if you have any questions, don't freeze up and try to think of a question on the spot. You either have one or you don't. Listening, rather than talking more than necessary, is always the way to go. I have winced on numerous occasions when an actor finished their audition and then negatively commented on it. I remember one actor ending his audition by stating, "Well that sucked!" Actually it didn't suck, but he convinced us, by his comment, that it did. Self-deprecation is not only indulgent, but a waste of everyone's time.

8. Very Obvious, But Worth Mentioning:

- Don't chew gum, unless that is specific character behavior.

- Be polite to EVERYONE!

- Don't be a high maintenance diva or a pain in the ass.

- Come across like you're a fun person to work with.

AUDITION HOT TIP #2

Try a Playful Approach. Instead of getting stressed when preparing for an audition/interview/meeting, choose to be enthusiastic. When you're upbeat, unburdened and open to possibility, it sets the stage for not taking anything, especially the entertainment industry, or yourself for that matter, too seriously. Enthusiasm translates into a feeling of lightness, which translates into the energy we, in casting, refer to as the "it" factor.

CHAPTER 3

PREPARATION EQUALS LIBERATION

I cannot stress enough the value of preparation. The competitive edge it gives the auditioning actor is priceless. The creative freedom it brings to the audition is essential to manifesting what those conducting the audition want to see. I am often asked what a casting director is looking for in an actor. The answer is simple. A casting director is looking for a prepared, actor who is likable, behaves professionally and who fits the character description of the role while bringing his or her energetic uniqueness to the text. And that applies across the board, whether you are up for a thirty-second toothpaste commercial, a day player part on a film or a leading role in a play. When you are prepared, you create a portal through which your artistic gifts can truly shine. All the information you can gather and absorb about the audition and role will relax and empower you. Most people put great thought into making plans if they are going to an important social or family event. They know certain arrangements need to be made such as reserving a hotel room or renting a tuxedo. These are basic, normal tasks a person takes on to prepare for a special occasion. Well, an argument can be made that any audition is a potentially special occasion for your acting career. Here then are some fundamental steps you can take to prepare for that audition/interview/meeting.

Get a Map

Your preparation should begin the moment you find out you have an audition. Make sure all the basics are covered, such as confirming the exact day, time, and location of your appointment. Ask if there is audition material or a script available ahead of time. If the material is from a play that is published, make it your business to buy and read it. If you're not sure how you should be dressed and whom you're auditioning for, ASK. Find out everything you can about the project. Learn as much as you can, approaching the whole experience as an inspiring opportunity, not a chore.

Using the great American play, "Death of a Salesman," the following is an example* of how to break a project down based on reading the script:

FULL TITLE · Death of a Salesman: Certain Private Conversations in Two Acts and a Requiem*

AUTHOR · Arthur Miller

TYPE OF WORK · Play

GENRE · Tragedy, social commentary, family drama

CLIMAX · The scene in Frank's Chop House and Biff's final confrontation with Willy at home

PROTAGONISTS · Willy Loman, Biff Loman

ANTAGONISTS · Biff Loman, Willy Loman, the American Dream

SETTING (TIME) · "Today," that is, the present; either the late 1940s or the time period in which the play is being produced, with "daydreams" into Willy's past; all of the action takes place during a twenty-four-hour period between Monday night and Tuesday night, except the "Requiem," which takes place, presumably, a few days after Willy's funeral

SETTING (PLACE) · According to the stage directions, "Willy Loman's house and yard [in Brooklyn] and . . . various places he visits in . . . New York and Boston"

FALLING ACTION · The "Requiem" section, although the play is not really structured as a classical drama

TENSE · Present

FORESHADOWING · Willy's flute theme foreshadows the revelation of his father's occupation and abandonment; Willy's preoccupation with Linda's stockings foreshadows his affair with The Woman; Willy's automobile accident before the start of Act I foreshadows his suicide at the end of Act II

TONE · The tone of Miller's stage directions and dialogue ranges from sincere to parodying, but, in general, the treatment is tender, though at times brutally honest, toward Willy's plight

THEMES · The American Dream; abandonment; betrayal

MOTIFS · Mythic figures; the American West; Alaska; the African jungle

SYMBOLS · Seeds; diamonds; Linda's and the woman's stockings; the rubber hose

(*Source: Sparknotes)

Listening to music and looking at photographs or films set in the period of the project plant strong creative subconscious seeds. If auditioning for a commercial, industrial or other project where the setting is more generic, like present day "any town" USA, then research general images as well as the specific features/benefits of the product or corporation for which you're auditioning.

AUDITION HOT TIP #3

Make your character likeable and/
or vulnerable, no matter what. One
of the benchmarks of a truly skilled
actor is to organically make the role
he or she is playing likeable. A few
of the clearest examples of this are:
Meryl Streep in "Doubt," Mickey
Rourke in "The Wrestler," Geoffrey
Rush's portrayal of the Marquis de
Sade in the film "Quills," Willem Dafoe
in "Spiderman," Anthony Hopkins as
Hannibal Lechter in "The Silence of the
Lambs," Charlize Theron in "Monster"
and Alan Arkin in "Little Miss Sunshine."

CHAPTER 4

THE TEXT IS YOUR FRIEND

In preparing effectively for an audition, the most helpful tool at an actor's disposal is the text. The text could be a full script, a stage play, a scene, monologue, commercial/industrial copy, improvisation guidelines, etc. When you get your audition appointment, ask what they'd like you to prepare. If it's not completely clear, this is also the time to ask where the character is from, his/her age and how you should be dressed. When you have your audition material in front of you don't give in to procrastination. Seize this opportunity to plan out your audition and come up with empowered, creative choices.

Regardless of its form (copy, script, play, monologue, synopsis, character description etc.), the text is a map leading to a treasure chest with a great audition waiting inside for you to discover. Planning your acting choices in advance is key, even if you get the material just moments before your audition begins. Upon receiving your sides or copy, the first step is to carefully read it in its entirety. Don't lose sight of the fact that the words have been deliberately selected by the writer. The manner in which you express and speak these words in your audition require the same consideration. Quick script analysis is a great way to begin your audition preparation and to explore choices. Take a highlighter and highlight all relevant words — anything that informs the character for which you're auditioning.

If you have a commercial audition, highlight all the words/sentences that name or refer to the product and its features. Then, place a plus sign or smiley face above them. This will prompt you to deliver these words/sentences with an upbeat, positive vocal and physical inflection.

Also highlight the words/sentences that name or refer to the product's competitor (such as Pepsi in the case of Coke) or a negative experience due to not using the advertised product (as in "My hands were so dry and cracked before I started using Gold Bond cream"). Above these highlighted words/sentences, put a minus sign or a sad face to cue a deflated vocal and physical inflection.

When auditioning for film/TV/stage, highlight your script or scene with the appropriate plus/minus signs or smiley/sad faces on the sections that convey the emotions of your character, or how your character feels about the person he/she is addressing in the scene.

In any type of audition, remember that verbs are action words and adjectives are modifiers that add color. So if you are saying a verb or adjective, match it emotionally with your voice. This will help bring an active, colorful liveliness to your audition performance. Write your acting objectives/reasons for every line or segment in the script to the point that you know, understand and believe what you're saying, why you are saying it and to whom.

AUDITION HOT TIP #4

Make a personal connection to the copy or sides. While you are reading the material, discover how your unique personal life experience relates to it. If your character is in a scene where he/she has lost a parent and you have not experienced that, then think of a loss you have actually gone through, like that of a grandparent or pet. The important thing is to immediately connect your humanity to the text.

CHAPTER 5

ICONIC SPECIFICITY™

Iconic specificity is a term I invented while teaching a cold reading workshop. It's a quick way to take a neutral read and color it energetically. This works especially well for commercial copy. I remember a thirty-second spot for a telephone company where the first line of the copy was "I'm a worrier." The actor auditioning delivered the line in a dull, flat way, which did not hold my attention. In having him do it again, I asked, "Who do you think is a notorious worrier?" He replied, "Woody Allen." "Perfect," I said. "Read the copy again and think, but don't imitate Woody Allen." He did it again, and this time his read was vastly improved, and he held my attention.

There's an irony here. Thinking of someone who is an "ICON" with a "SPECIFIC" manner freed the actor and allowed some of his own individual sparkle to come through the audition.

Another example involved an actor auditioning for a Pizza chain commercial promoting "New York" style pizza. The actor's first read was predictably bland. Before the second take I asked the actor to name someone he considered to be a well-known New Yorker. He answered, "Donald Trump." I said, "Don't impersonate Donald Trump, but think, breathe and feel his spirit coming through you." His second read had absolutely no resemblance to how Donald Trump sounds or acts, but it was driven by a sharp, magnetic, New York City-like energy that resulted in a callback.

Drawing upon a mental and energetic blueprint of a specific icon (i.e.

Marilyn Monroe or your Uncle Jimmy), allows your subconscious mind to help you get out of your way. Being anchored in a specific image enables you to deliver an energetic, interesting and engaging audition.

Try it for yourself, and you'll feel the difference. First, take the copy and read it without anyone specific in mind. Then, do it again after you have answered the following questions:

Iconic Specificity™ Check List

1) Is the copy specific to a geographic location?

2) Where is my character from and what does he/she sound like?

3) What personality traits, based on the copy, does/ could my character have?

4) Which icon or person (that I am familiar with) shares these character traits?

5) What is my character's occupation?

AUDITION HOT TIP #5

Don't play the pauses. Timing
and pacing is everything when it
comes to delivering copy. Don't
consciously play pauses between
words, sentences or thoughts. Don't
savor each word as if it was an exotic
delicacy nor rush through like you
can't wait to escape the audition.
Instead, connect to the natural flow of
breath when you are speaking.

CHAPTER 6

THE MOMENT BEFORE AND
THE MOMENT AFTER –
PUTTING YOUR AUDITION IN A FRAME

A simple, effective way to instantly add spark to your audition is to both start and end with a quick moment of physical action. These actions are typically referred to as a "moment before" and a "button". It's as if you silently yet energetically become the first and last beat of the copy. Employing this technique enables you to frame your audition and bring focus to it. For the first part, take a few seconds (and I stress FEW) before you actually speak to perform an action relevant to the role and text. This instantly draws the attention of those who are auditioning you. But it is essential to be brief and specific.

To illustrate this more specifically, let's say you're delivering commercial copy for a pain reliever. A good moment before would be to have your eyes closed and head tilted to the side supported by one hand. This three-second moment sets the tone and puts you, the actor in charge. It quickly conveys/ suggests to those for whom you are auditioning that you are in pain and need relief. Of course, the relief naturally comes from the pain reliever's miraculous healing powers. That's because, in commercial land, the product advertised is God and Master of the Universe. This leads into the second part of this framing technique, the moment after or "button."

When delivering the last line of copy always end on the upbeat. In other words, be sure your vocal inflection rises on the last line. This makes your final impression positive.

Though not mandatory, you may also want to add a physical gesture. If you do add physical business at the end, make it real and organic, not fake (i.e. winking, finger pointing etc.). Working in much the same way as a frame around a picture, accentuating the beginning and end of your audition allows you and the material to stand out.

AUDITION HOT TIP #6

With commercial copy, always
physically smile when you say
the name of the product being
advertised. This reinforces the positive,
winning tone of your delivery and
automatically makes you likeable.

CHAPTER 7

"NICE" EQUALS "NEXT" – MAKING YOUR SECOND TAKE YOUR FIRST

Playing it safe is a poor audition choice and a waste of your most valuable resource, namely YOU. Many actors fail to take risks in their auditions because of an uncertainty regarding what the casting director is looking for. But there's nothing to be uncertain about. Let me assure you, the casting director is looking for the best person for the part. End of story. It is not up to those who are conducting the audition to spoon-feed you exactly what they're after. If they knew specifically, to the last detail, what they wanted, the need for casting would be eliminated.

Society expects adults of sound mind to be responsible and accountable for their actions. The casting director expects actors to take control of every detail of their audition. Your preparation, grooming, attention to detail, wardrobe, getting enough sleep, getting extra help from a coach if needed -- these are all choices to consider. If you are fortunate enough to get an audition appointment, assume you have already earned the casting director's respect. Though the casting director is on your side, make no mistake: expectations are high. Casting directors need actors who are not only talented, but also professional, well-groomed, prepared and fun to work with. Anything less makes a casting director look bad to their clients, and that could threaten future business.

If it takes you a little while to get warmed up and relaxed then, by all means, do what you have to do. Eat, breathe, sleep, and drink the character. Work out, meditate, do whatever it takes to get to your best place internally. Like an athlete preparing for a sporting event, the goal is to be ready to go at the appointed time. That separates the professionals from the wanna-bes.

Your audition preparation is more than just showing up on time. I remember a theatre and film director with whom I regularly work once lamenting about actors who traveled from New York City to Connecticut for an EPA (Equity Principal Audition) open call. He couldn't understand why so many of these actors made the effort to travel such a long way to audition, but put little effort into the quality of their auditions.

Please don't think it's enough to just show up. We are so fortunate to be in an industry where live human interaction is still a priority. Face time is valuable, and wasting an industry professional's time with a boring, neutral audition is unproductive for everyone. So, keep this in mind: if "Nice" equals "Next" then "Preparation equals Liberation".

Create a Detail Checklist for yourself. Take inventory of your character's aspects. Fine attention to detail is the sign of a prepared actor. The following list is helpful for legit auditions (film/TV/stage) much the same way that the Iconic Specificity checklist is a proven, useful tool for commercial auditions.

Detail Check List

Character Name:

Age:

Physical type:

Ethnicity:

Where he/she grew up:

Profession:

Clothing style:

Who he/she is speaking to:

What he/she wants:

Why he/she is here:

What he/she is doing:

Drawing from anyone you know personally or otherwise, this character reminds you of:

AUDITION HOT TIP #7

If the casting director asks you a
question or gives you an adjustment,
that is usually a good thing. It often
means there is interest in knowing
more about you or seeing how well
you take direction. If you are given
an adjustment make sure you listen to
the direction carefully and follow it.
Responding to an adjustment with the
same exact read is the kiss of death.
What it says to the casting director
is you have no levels and don't take
direction well. Also, in answering any
questions, always respond politely,
intelligently and above all, with
confidence.

CHAPTER 8

THE 3 P'S –
PROFESSIONALISM, PRESENTATION AND
PROTOCOL

Manners are important in all situations especially professional ones. How you behave and interact with your colleagues, peers, industry professionals etc., can have a huge impact on whether or not you book a job.

This true story is a perfect example.

I was in a callback session for a feature film my office was casting. The director, producer, my associate and myself were in the studio. An actor who had a callback appointment gave a top-notch audition. He was prepared, looked great, understood the script, became the character before our eyes, acted the hell out of the scene and was a lot of fun. As a result, we all knew we wanted to hire him. When he exited the room, we had a conversation, sharing our enthusiastic comments about his amazing audition.

About a half-hour later, another casting director, working in the same facility on a different project asked to speak with me. It turned out when she was walking down the hall earlier, she saw our "fabulous" actor leaning his ear on the door to my studio in an attempt to eavesdrop on our PRIVATE conversation about him. When this casting director confronted the actor, he quickly gave an excuse and made a hasty exit into the elevator. When my director and producer heard about this incident, major doubts were placed in their minds about casting him. They did not want to risk hiring an actor who was potentially shady.

Long story short, because of his bad behavior, he ended up losing a role he had earned on the strength of his audition. I will never dislike anyone for being overly ambitious, but being duplicitous never pays off. Understand you have no control over the outcome of the audition, so it's always best to let it go and move on.

Actors are always telling me they don't know the proper protocol when meeting industry professionals. It's really simple. If you know how to behave around people you must respect, i.e. grandparents, bosses etc., then you know how to conduct yourself within the industry. When you show others respect, you show that you clearly respect yourself, and that's where it all starts. Part of that showing of respect is to have your picture and resume with you in case it's requested. Being courteous to EVERYONE says a lot of positive things about you as a professional. Conversely, an attitude can bite you in the butt. This industry is close knit, and everybody talks. Any rudeness taking place outside of the audition room will likely be noted by someone and eventually reach the ears of those deciding who to hire. And bad behavior can haunt and hurt your career for years as today's assistant often becomes tomorrow's casting director, agent or producer. So do yourself a favor: DON'T BE A FREAKIN' DIVA.

When you are inside the casting studio, your goal is to work the room, not our nerves. As I mentioned earlier, if you have a bag, set it by the door so you won't forget it. Greet everyone with a smile and thank them for seeing you. Listen carefully to any instructions or direction you are given. If you have a RELEVANT question, by all means ask it. The casting director is there to help and support you. When you've finished the audition and nothing else is asked of you, thank everyone again, wish them a good rest of the day, grab your bag and go. Don't stand there and ramble or discuss your performance as this will diminish the impact of you and your audition. It's like standing in a bed of quicksand; the longer you remain, the more your chances sink. Exit with a smile and your head held high, knowing that regardless of what transpires here, there's always next time.

AUDITION HOT TIP #8

Connect to the audition reader. If your audition material involves more than yourself, it is likely an audition reader will be provided. Remember, the reader is there to support your audition by providing a human presence to whom you can respond and react. Before you start, connect to the audition reader with your eyes and thank him/her. This brief, positive act of courtesy will encourage the reader (even if only subconsciously) to be on your side. You can further empower your audition by imagining an invisible cord linking you to the reader. Avoid, at all cost, projecting a dismissive attitude toward the reader for this will only promote resentment and make your audition more difficult. Try to be an audition reader yourself to gain invaluable insight.

CHAPTER 9

SOMETIMES EAST IS WEST AND LESS IS MORE – PLAYING THE UNEXPECTED

Acting choices are an essential part of your audition preparation. One of the most helpful tools you will have at your disposal and one that can apply to any scenario is choosing to play the opposite of what's expected. In making such a choice, take the time to creatively experiment, allowing the discovery process to unfold and give you control. It will show the casting director that you know how to think outside of the box and be engaging. With practice, you will see for yourself that the more interesting choices are often the less obvious ones. Take inventory (based on the script/sides/copy) of the obvious choices and the opposite or less obvious choices that your character could make. Try this for your next audition and see how your choices become transformed.

Obvious/Less Obvious Choice Inventory

Take a sheet of paper and divide it into two columns. Head the left column "Obvious Choices" and the right column "Opposite or Less Obvious Choices." Scrutinizing your audition material this way lets you get deeper inside the character.

Choice Work Sheet

Line:

Obvious Choice:

Effect:

Opposite/Less Obvious Choice:

Effect:

Here is an example:

Line: *"I'm not crazy."*

Obvious Choice: *Screaming the line loudly and defensively.*

Effect: *Predictable and grating.*

Opposite/Less Obvious Choice: *Delivering the line in a soft voice with a smile.*

Effect: *Surprising and interesting enough to get a callback.*

Enjoy this part of the process, and be inspired. The creative freedom of preparation diffuses nervousness and insecurity.

A prepared actor is appreciated by the industry. He/she is showing a mutual respect and professionalism and will be remembered for future casting calls. Understand that from the perspective of the casting director, producer or director, there is no reason to use actors who don't show anything special.

AUDITION HOT TIP #9

Be aware of balance. An over-prepared actor leaves no room for direction or spontaneity and usually comes across as rigid. Trust yourself to know when you've done the work and combine that readiness with a willingness to be free and open.

CHAPTER 10

THE COPY AS PROP –
YOUR SECURITY BLANKET AND OTHER
GREAT USES

Generally, most auditions utilize copy or sides. In the case of commercial or industrial auditions, cue cards are normally provided. Actors often ask if it's better to have the material fully memorized. I believe it is to your advantage to know and understand the copy extremely well. The more comfortable you are with it, the better. If you have been given sides and cue cards are not part of the audition, come in with your copy. Concern over "not getting the words right" will be minimized because you have the safety net of the material being in your hands. It is more important to get to the heart and truth of the character than to micro-manage every word. During preparation, once you know the sides by heart, play around by incorporating the copy as a prop and putting it in the scene. This is an inventive, resourceful and cool way to add detail and creativity. It also comes across as very empowering.

Here is an example: An actor came in for a callback on a play I was casting. The scene he was reading took place in a bar. He had the scene memorized, yet he entered with the audition material in hand. As the scene began, he rolled the sides into a cylinder and used that cylinder as a glass from which the character was drinking. This transformation of the sides into a prop, enhanced the moment beautifully. The actor was prepared, extremely gifted, very professional and able to demonstrate creativity and a great sense of humor. Bottom line, he got the part.

Learn your audition material to the point that you technically don't need to refer to it, but have it with you in the audition in case you do. You will feel less vulnerable and more in control if you work in some physical business with the sides. Experiment with the endless possibilities. Here are a few examples I have seen in auditions: menu, umbrella, newspaper, tennis racket, gun, dagger, wait staff pad, cop pad, school book, rolling pin – you get the picture. Have fun and play!

AUDITION HOT TIP #10

Think about the audience. Once you have identified all the aspects of the role you're playing, contemplate what expectations you would have of this role if you were in the audience. If you have an audition for a comedy or a humorous commercial, the audience expectation would be to have fun and laugh. Considering what the casting director expects will add more depth to your audition.

CHAPTER 11:

YOU ARE WHAT YOU WEAR

This may seem an obvious statement but many actors fail to realize how crucial common sense is to their auditions. I cannot stress enough how everything informing your performance should come from the writing, including your wardrobe. Learning to balance the subtle details can really enhance an audition and contribute significantly toward making a positive impact. By the same token, not having a good grasp in this area can be disastrous.

Case in point: I was teaching a workshop, and the actor presenting her monologue, though well-dressed, was hiding behind a shopping bag crammed with unnecessary props. I knew she was nervous as she was randomly digging into the bag, awkwardly pulling out prop after prop, and not knowing where to put anything. She struggled with the lines, and it was clear she was working from the outside in. She did not know the monologue well enough to even consider using props. Yet here she was awash in them.

Another time, an actor was auditioning for a film, where the role was that of a criminal. He wore a business suit and pulled out a real knife. I was taken off guard, (not in a good way) and put off. Using dangerous props for shock value only makes a bad impression and is disrespectful to the casting director. I will never call this actor in for any more auditions. Not only was he dressed inappropriately for the role, he was using an illegal weapon as a prop.

Shoes and hem length can be especially distracting and not for the right reasons. I've seen actresses give perfectly fine auditions only to lose my attention to shoes belonging only around a stripper pole.

Ladies, if you are wearing a dress or skirt for your audition and you are seated, please remember the voice of your mother or guardian saying, "Close your legs please! That's a free show we don't want to see."

When you hear about your audition, whether you got the appointment on your own or through a talent representative, you need to ask how you should dress if you were not already told (refer to Ch. 7, Detail Check List). Remember, it is your responsibility to prepare yourself from the inside out.

Some examples of applying detail to wardrobe choices are:

WAIT STAFF/FOOD SERVER · Black pants, white shirt, pen placed over your ear, use your copy as a dupe pad.

DOCTOR/SCIENTIST · Neutral top and pants, layered with a borrowed lab coat. Your sides attached to a clipboard is a nice touch.

OFFICER · Black or navy pants with matching shirt, use your copy as a pad.

Long skirts are great for period pieces.

CONSTRUCTION WORKER · T-shirt, jeans, work boots, bandanna, borrowed tool belt.

While watching a film, play, TV show, or commercial, take note of the costumes and why the characters are wearing them. There are no random or arbitrary choices in professional productions. Wardrobe, like props and actions, provide the audience with visual cues about who this character is in relation to the story.

Build an audition wardrobe. Clothing should be functional and also convey a sense of the character you're auditioning for. Take an inventory of your clothes, shoes and accessories and sort them into categories according to role and era.

A few category examples are: Upscale & Formal, Business Professional, Urban, Rural, Middle Class, Working Class, Blue Collar, The Working Poor, Unemployed, Educated, Uneducated etc. Once you know the specific role for which you are auditioning, you can then make informed audition wardrobe choices based on who the character is and what he/she would wear in the situation depicted.

AUDITION HOT TIP #11

You are the filter. Have you ever brewed a cup of coffee without a filter? If you have, you know the result is a hot mess of terrible tasting coffee. Be aware of the role your individual humanity plays in "filtering" the character you are auditioning for. Explore ways of including yourself in the mix.

CHAPTER 12

NOBODY WANTS TO WORK WITH CRAZY

In the Business of Acting class I teach, one of my favorite sections is called, "Crazy S#&* I Get in The Mail." Part of this section entails showing actual pictures and resumes sent to my office from actors who are clueless about marketing themselves.

From all that I've experienced in this business, I've come to believe that there are basically two kinds of actors. There's the artist who will act no matter what because it is his/her vocation, soul and craft. And then there are those who want to be famous, who are likely starved for love and attention and will do anything and/or anybody to get what they want. It seems this second type is, unfortunately, in the majority.

I estimate that fewer than 5% of the total acting pool are truly talented artists with amazing gifts and technical skill. The truth is there are far too many people who believe they want to be actors, but aren't very good at it. This is why the same group of exceptional actors who share a similar type often run into each other at auditions.

In this field, self-confidence and being physically and mentally healthy are musts. Leave any attitude, neurosis, and emotional baggage at home. Far too often, I have met actors who come across as desperate, needy, creepy, slutty, defeated, suicidal, angry, self-deprecating and entitled; or I have received their marketing materials reflecting the same. Dealing with an unstable person who believes he/she is an actor can be sad, uncomfortable and sometimes dangerous.

Even little things like email addresses can be quite revealing. I have received emails from addresses like: **Hotbabygirl@_____.com, Ready4U@_____.com, and 420Blunt@_____.com**. Clearly, these are actors who have a lot on their plate, a plate from which I don't wish to be served.

With email addresses and all other aspects, separate your personal life from your professional life. It takes only seconds to set up an email account for all matters concerning your acting career. Many actors simply use their first initial and last name for their email address (J.SmithActor@gmail.com). I recommend Gmail as it's free, works universally and has great storage as well as recovery capabilities.

How you conduct yourself at the audition can say a lot about you (see Ch.8 The 3 P's). Were you rude and demanding? Were you critical or annoying? Were you respectful of the people around you? Were you such a prepared "method actor," so deep in character that you couldn't give the casting director any eye contact? Did you act as if the audition reader was your servant? Did you give a rambling, self-indulgent speech (that no one wanted to hear) before your audition about why you were late? Be mindful of your behavior. You may get a callback on the strength of your audition, but you may not get hired if you come across like a loon.

AUDITION HOT TIP #12

Have a Day Dream

Once you've determined who your character is, what acting choices you'll be making, what you'll be doing with the copy, etc., have a conscious vision of your ideal audition. Be as specific, positive, energetic and imaginative as possible. See and feel the casting and production team as kind, fun, good people. See yourself as feeling and looking your best and giving a top-notch audition. This is a terrific way to positively feed your subconscious mind and give yourself confidence from within.

CHAPTER 13

WHAT'S MY STORY?

In addition to gathering details about the role for which you're auditioning (see Detail Check List, Chapter 7), developing a mini biography or back-story gives you a point of origin. For any audition, ask yourself these three simple questions:

1) Who am I?

2) What is my relationship to the person I'm addressing or to the audience?

3) How did I arrive at the circumstances I find myself in?

The answers you come up with for these questions will help put your read in a specific, individualized context.

I was casting a filmed dramatization of a historical event for a documentary. One actor came in to audition and gave a very flat, boring read. On top of that, I could barely hear him. When I asked him the same three questions listed above, he responded with a blank stare. Shifting uncomfortably, he then began to sweat and stammer. When I gently explained I wasn't putting him on the spot but wanted to help him, he was able to respond with: 1) "I'm a union organizer, 2) I am at a secret meeting, and I want to convince the workers to unite. 3) I lost loved ones to unfair, inhumane treatment in the sweatshops, and I'm fighting for their honor."

Delivering the read a second time, he transformed into the character, and I believed him. As an artist, take the opportunity to dig deep into the character you're breathing life into. Regardless of whether you have six lines or six pages of dialogue, sketch out the life and arc of the character you are up for. And apply that sketch to your audition. Come up with at least a paragraph or two about your character's life. When choosing where the character is from and how they sound vocally, make sure everything supports the copy and what the casting director is looking for. This is especially important regarding commercials and where they will be airing. Tacking on an accent for sheer effect could ruin the audition. It is imperative that all character details are consistent and credible with the text.

Example 1:
Commercial copy for "Divine Chocolate Delights," Role: MOM

START · "As a busy Mom, I love the nutritional benefits, and individual fresh packs of Divine Chocolate Delights. My kids just love the taste – Oh yeah – so do I, simply heavenly." END

CHARACTER BIO · I'm a 34-year old working mother of two from Connecticut. I'm president of the PTA , have a great sense of humor, and I know how to juggle family and work. I love baking for the family, but when I'm too busy, I serve Divine Chocolate Delights. I trust the fresh ingredients, the convenient individual packaging and the taste. I'm a bit of a chocolate fiend, and this tames the wild beast in me every time.

This bio ties into the features of the product, which is what you're selling. Allow such biographical details to fuel your audition by infusing them into your mindset, persona and presentation of the character.

With a legit audition (film, TV, stage), you can be more layered and creative.

Example 2:
Day Player copy for prime time cop TV series, Role: THUG

START · "I didn't do it man, don't touch me or I'll cut you! Go ahead and shoot me, you damn pigs are all alike." END

CHARACTER BIO · I'm a 20-year old young man raised in an abusive household in the Bronx. In and out of foster care since I was three, I was told my whole life that I'm worthless. I was sent to a group home when I was fourteen and haven't lived in a real house since. I know what it's like to go to sleep hungry on a park bench and to sell myself for a little crack. I don't care what happens to me since no one else gives a damn.

Putting a little effort into a back-story can add a surprising level of sensitivity and vulnerability into what would otherwise be another predictable character stereotype.

AUDITION HOT TIP #13

Get trained in I.P.A.

I.P.A. or the International Phonetic Alphabet is a system that breaks down all the sounds of the English language into symbols. By making you familiar with stress and intonation patterns, it provides a solid technical base for learning practically any dialect. Having this training broadens your opportunities, especially if your look warrants playing various cultures.

CHAPTER 14

IMPROVISATION —
LOOKS EASY, BUT IT'S NOT

Improvisation or improv as it's commonly known is any performance that spontaneously creates specific characters in particular situations. In this process, the actor relies on personal experience, knowledge and instincts. Inventiveness is key as the performer has no preparation. An audience is often involved, offering the actor or actors suggestions and specific details to follow.

Improvisation is an art form and skill to be mastered. Many inexperienced actors assume it's an easy way out because there are no lines to memorize. But this is a false assumption. Training in improvisation will teach you how to develop characters quickly, think on your feet, and trust the other actors with whom you're working. These tools are an asset in any audition.

Taking an improv class or being a member of an improv troupe exercises your acting muscles in deep and creative ways. Think of it as a workout for your acting body. Some of the most brilliant and successful actors today (especially those gifted in comedy) have roots in the improv world. Vince Vaughn, Ben Stiller, Will Ferrell, Robin Williams, Christopher Guest, Amy Poehler, Martin Short, Andrea Martin, and Wayne Brady are a few who immediately come to mind.

Rent films or TV shows known for their cast of outstanding improvisers. For instance: any season of Curb Your Enthusiasm, Who's Line is it Anyway and Second City (SCTV); any film directed by

Robert Altman or Woody Allen; "The Break Up" with Vince Vaughn and Jennifer Aniston, "Waiting for Guffman," "Best in Show," "A Mighty Wind," "For Your Consideration" and of course, the classic "This is Spinal Tap." Explore YouTube and other sites on the internet for more obscure offerings.

As part of your training go to improv shows and soak it all in as an audience member. See firsthand how the actors on stage demonstrate absolute trust with themselves and each other, while receiving audience input. Improvisation is truly a collaborative art, teaching actors to listen well, be in the moment and work in the spirit of mutual respect (rather than the typical every person for him/herself attitude). That's because improvisation promotes the craft of actors depending on and supporting each other in a scene.

It may seem an irony or paradox (life is full of them), but being a selfish actor ultimately doesn't serve yourself or your audition. On the other hand, the more you give to your fellow actor, the better both of you look.

Do whatever it takes to experience what it feels like to act with your imagination. Lack of funds or time is no excuse. Volunteer or barter time in exchange for classes. Be an usher at a theatre to get behind the scenes and see shows for free. You'd be surprised how often asking for this kind of arrangement provides opportunities to enhance and grow your career. It all comes down to this: If you want something badly enough, you'll find a way to get it.

AUDITION HOT TIP #14

Let those who are conducting the audition "see" you listening. If you are on stage or in the shot (regardless of whether or not you are speaking), you are in character and need to stay there. The next time you are watching a really good play, film or TV show, take notice of the actors who are not speaking. See how they act without saying a word. Observe how they support their fellow actors. Volumes can be revealed through a mere gesture or facial expression. There is good reason why Academy Awards are given for the best supporting actor/actress.

CHAPTER 15

THEATRE = 10, FILM = 5
WALKING THE BOARDS vs
PLAYING TO THE LENS

While many stage actors have come to me asking how they can format their auditions for film and TV, just as many film/TV actors ask for tips on how to step up their game for stage auditions. Here, I caution all actors not to over-analyze as this can become a case (as Shakespeare brilliantly put it) of "Much Ado About Nothing." The approach I recommend is to regard every type of audition as its own separate and unique acting style, of which there are many.

These styles require certain modifications when auditioning. Consider the various styles of theatre, for example. In performing the Greek Classics, Restoration, Commedia del Arte, Shakespeare, Pinter, Mamet, etc., there are very real technical and stylistic differences. Likewise, within Film, TV and other performance mediums, there are multiple ways to go, multiple schools of expression. What I suggest is that you zero in on the style that seems most appropriate for whatever kind of audition you may have.

Commercial, Soap Opera, Film, Episodic TV Drama, Situation Comedy, Theatre (Dramatic & Comedic), Musical Theatre, etc.- all have their respective technical requirements. Applying simple, relevant, stylistic adjustments to your audition insures a solid foundation to build upon.

The following is a breakdown of the major audition acting categories or styles and quick tips on how to instantly enhance them.

THEATRE

Play to the back of the house. On a scale of 1-10, your intensity level and volume should be at least 8. Gauge the size of the audition space. If you are in a small studio, the intensity level and volume should be at 5 or 6. If your audition is in an actual theatre, then your levels need to be at 10.

Don't live in the chair. When your audition scene has your character in a chair, make sure you find a point where you can get up (unless it is specified in the sides that the character is to remain seated). Your body will instinctively know on it's own when to stand. Trust yourself. During preparation, make the decision that you will get up before the end of the scene, but don't specify when, and see what happens. This subtle action will grab and hold the casting director's attention and keep the energy moving.

MUSICAL THEATRE

Preparation and attitude are everything; these auditions can't be phoned in.

- Make sure you are upbeat and smiling.

- Never sing with your eyes closed. It disconnects you and looks self-indulgent.

- Being well-dressed and groomed is standard musical theatre audition protocol.

- Make sure your songbook is up to date, neat and legible for the accompanist.

- Warm up prior to your audition; you must be in good voice.

FILM/TV DRAMA

Put yourself in frame. Where the intensity level for stage is a 10, the appropriate energy level for Film and TV drama would be around 5. That's because the camera lens magnifies everything it views. A good, general rule of thumb is to contain your intensity to about half of what you would bring to a theatre audition. Maintain an intimacy with the camera. Imagine yourself framed in the camera shot, emanating the character and connecting through the eyes.

TELEVISION/ SITCOM

Put your intensity level around 8.

Be somewhat bold and slightly broad with your physicality. The TV comedy world is a heightened and exaggerated reality.

Don't compete with the words; let them flow and lead you to a natural rhythm of delivery. Timing is everything.

Play the comedy straight (see Ch. 9, Playing the Opposite). The inherent humor of comedic situations can reach their greatest levels of funny when played seriously.

SOAP OPERA

Put your intensity level around 6.

Become comfortable with learning material and blocking rapidly. If you struggle with memorization, the soap world is not for you. This genre is extremely fast-paced, and if hired you are expected to learn voluminous amounts quickly as Soap Opera dialogue is the primary means of moving the story line along. Make the ridiculous natural. Many soap plots are extreme and insane. Believe every line you're saying as the absolute truth.

COMMERCIALS

Put your intensity level around 7.

Every word, breath, and action counts. There are no minor details in commercials.

Have your character believe that the product being advertised is the answer to all of life's problems.

AUDITION HOT TIP #15

Give yourself a sensory rehearsal. Find a way to connect your senses to the project for which you're auditioning. Regarding commercials, if you're able to see and experience the product being advertised up close, do so. If your character is in a specific environment, put yourself there by renting a DVD, searching online or going outside. Get your senses involved and yourself engaged; inhale and feel your way into the character.

CHAPTER 16

IT'S NOW OR NEVER –
BEING "IN THE MOMENT" AND STAYING THERE

As a mother of two kids there is one statement I find myself repeating often to them: "The most important thing is right now." I believe this applies universally. Being in the moment is necessary in auditions because it keeps you centered and aware of what you are doing. Practice being in the present moment as often as possible. Every time you speak a word in the script or copy, come from a place of spontaneous discovery as if it's the first time you've ever said these words.

To get beneath the surface of the words, a helpful exercise is to write your character's objective/reason/intention for every line. You need to consciously and unconsciously understand what your character is saying and why they're saying it. Don't be afraid to show vulnerability (see Ch. 13, What's My Story) when it applies to the text.

Showing a true range of authentic human emotions gives your audition depth and keeps it from becoming dull. Don't be overly dramatic and drag out every word. Trust that the material is good and is written to flow as naturally as possible. Falling into the trap of pausing for effect or physically indicating moments will give you an unnatural result. Any artificial, fake physical business, i.e. pointing, winking, is indicating. Gesturing to an object or person in the scene, or to the audience is a common mistake (unless, of course, it is a stage direction). Make sure you can identify your character's environment, the time of day, and what they are doing. Find ways of personalizing your audition. A simple detail, like a small prop used in accordance with the copy, can make a huge difference.

An actor I spoke to recently told me she booked a huge job. In our conversation, it came out that she had done something special in her audition. Based on who her character was, she incorporated the use of a lollipop in the scene. This choice was validated by the script, and it brought the role to life. More than that, it helped her land a great gig.

In legit auditions, sometimes more than one scene is required to reflect the character's arc or personal journey. To show the beginning of the journey and a transition, you can draw upon simple, but effective tricks that utilize hairstyle and wardrobe. For example, in the earlier scene, to show more innocence prior to a transformation, the actor could be wearing hair up or in a ponytail (for a female) or combed out (for a male). Then the ponytail could be let out (female) or slicked back (male) for the scene after the character has transitioned.

Clothing is also very effective in showing a character's development. Having a jacket or sweater on for one scene and then removing it for another can be revealing about the character and indicate a strong choice. Such creative details, coupled with a little imagination, make a huge difference and could get you that callback.

AUDITION HOT TIP #16

Act as if your character has a surprise or secret.

No matter what kind of audition it is, identify a secret or surprise your character may have. Don't reveal, nor be literal about it, just feel the possibilities. This exercise can serve up great energy.

Say you're auditioning for a food commercial. Your character's secret could be that he/she just had a romantic rendezvous. Merely thinking about this can bring forth a sensual energy that carries over into the audition and creates the impression that the character really loves the taste of the advertised food.

CHAPTER 17

WHY YOU WON'T GET THE JOB –
THE CASTING MAZE IS A MINEFIELD

The audition appointment schedule is a most frustrating mathematical equation that many actors simply don't understand.

Depending on the project, a casting director can see only 40-80 actors per day. But, on average, submissions for about 10 times that amount are received and considered. This gives you a sense of how extremely selective casting directors are in this buyer's market. As contenders, you want to do all that you can to be remembered as an actor who is inspiring, gifted, fun, professional and easy-going. Any lack of professionalism, rudeness, poor preparation, etc. are reasons to not be called in for future auditions (see Chapter 8, The 3 P's). With so many talented, hard-working actors who would love the opportunity to get an audition appointment, it is a tragedy when another actor (who doesn't care enough about him/herself, the project or the people involved) squanders that opportunity.

Here's another paradox of the audition process: You should make the preparation for your audition about you, yet surrender (once you arrive for your audition) to the forces beyond your control.

In previous chapters, I've cited several examples of how actors sabotage their auditions. If you remember only one thing from this book, let it be this: an actor gets the job because of an ability to allow amazing artistry and skill to come through in the audition.

Though the auditioning system isn't perfect (what is?), it largely succeeds in identifying the best talent as the cream truly rises to the top.

Many brilliant actors are forgiven their poor behavior, addictions and bad judgment because their gifts are transcendent when they act. This may sound harsh, but truly inspiring, gifted actors are few and far between. So, if an actor's talent is suppressed during the audition, you can't fault the casting director or producer or director for not seeing it.

View your acting career as the Olympics. Train, learn from your experiences, grow and go for the gold. Be open and refrain from judging too quickly or harshly because you never know where the next great opportunity will appear. Good, professional, consistent and sane actors are a reliable source of talent and will receive the most audition opportunities. Agents, managers and casting directors are always looking to add new faces to their talent pool. You just need to give them good reasons to add you. For a casting director, in particular, the infusion of fresh sources of talent is absolutely essential to staying competitive and getting hired for new projects.

When you find yourself in a situation within the industry (be it a professional or social setting), use this opportunity to express your uniqueness and make a positive, memorable impression. Actors often speak of networking, which is a term I am personally not fond of. It is a "necessary evil" in this business, often driven solely by how one can profit, career-wise, from someone using someone else. I personally prefer the more meaningful method of developing long-term alliances, which by nature is more reciprocal.

There is so much inherent mistrust in the industry that the best collaborations (certainly the most meaningful ones) are usually among trusted friends. Most of the projects I cast and produce are done through repeat business or a referral. I find it obviously transparent and uncomfortable when an actor comes up to me practically salivating because they think I'm going to get them work. Ironically, the actors I end up helping and supporting the most are the ones who don't ask for my help.

AUDITION HOT TIP #17

In show business, as elsewhere, this time-worn adage applies: Keep your friends close and your enemies closer. The entertainment industry attracts some eccentric, dramatic people. There are artists and business professionals competing and co-existing within a very tight and desperate market place. In many ways, it's akin to a private club that doesn't want new members. Keep your negative opinions about others in the business to yourself. You could be overheard gossiping about an agent or director only to have that malice repeated and amplified by others. Careers rise and fall everyday, so the power structure is always changing. Be forthright and kind to everyone. Leave the negativity to others.

CHAPTER 18

MARKETING 101 - KNOW THYSELF

You are a product, a specific brand. When marketing yourself, possessing clarity of who you are and how that knowledge translates into casting is pivotal. I encourage acting students to enjoy the roles they play in conservatory or university productions as this will likely be the only time they're able to stretch their acting muscles outside of their age range. It is inspiring to see a 20-year old college junior beautifully play the role of a 60-year old.

Casting is an extremely subjective and contradictory process. Outside of school and voiceovers, being the right type for the role is often half the battle for the actor. While knowing your casting age range and type is essential, you also need the best marketing tools possible. A proper acting resume is a must no matter what your level of experience (see resource list for books that can help). Your headshot is your calling card and should realistically look like you on a good day. Most actors use two headshots – one for legit (film/TV/stage) and one for commercial work.

A legit shot should make a visual statement about you. More than just taking a picture of your physical self, the camera is also capturing your energetic self. This is why headshots need to be updated every so often. If you are very young, your picture needs to be updated more often as you are changing and growing with every new life experience. When you are older, if you haven't had any radical changes such as a drastic haircut or a major shift in weight, your headshot can have a longer shelf life. Also, your headshot needs to be in color; the days of black and white are now archaic.

For commercials, your image has to be associated with the branding and marketing of a product. Smiling is a must in a commercial headshot. If you have issues with smiling, if you are uncomfortable with your teeth, deal with it. Cosmetic dentistry is a beautiful thing. Practice smiling in the mirror and make it second nature. As part of a commercial audition, it is common procedure to have a snapshot taken of you smiling. So, there's no point in being self-conscious.

For the best results, make sure your picture is taken by a professional headshot photographer, as they have the expertise required to give you what you need. Consult with several, and see who you connect with and trust before making a decision. And never pay for a consultation; this should be free; look at it as the photographer's audition to get hired by you. In all instances, use your common sense as a consumer.

Your resume should reflect your training and experience truthfully and in the most positive light. It must be in the proper format and easy to read. Make sure both your cell number and email are listed. Never include your age range as this will be determined by the casting director at the audition. An age range is usually a 5-10 year span going younger to older. The younger you are, the tighter the range. A child, depending on size and look, might play 6-8 years old, while an older actor, depending on look, wardrobe and circumstances of the character, could possibly play mid 30's to early 40's. Ask people you know and don't know how old they think you are to get a sense of the age range you could play.

Identify the types of roles and projects that touch and inspire you. If commercials or soap operas don't do it for you, set them aside and focus on what you're passionate about.

AUDITION HOT TIP #18

Whenever you watch TV, you have an opportunity to take a free acting class. Whether it's a program or a commercial, take in every detail. Try to deconstruct what you're watching by asking yourself, "Why did this actor get hired?" "How did he or she read the copy?" "What was the actor doing physically?" Have a notebook on hand and jot down notes about what you liked or disliked about the performance. Identify which "tricks" you could "borrow" and apply to your auditions.

CHAPTER 19

FAITH OR FEAR –
WHICH DO YOU BRING WHEN YOU
WALK INTO THE ROOM?

Having an internal trust in yourself and your skills is a necessary anchor in the audition process. The degree of preparation needed will vary based on how much you allow who you are to be present at the heart and soul of every audition, interview or meeting. Give yourself permission to tell your artistic story through the work.

Regardless of your personal beliefs, find ways of accessing your spiritual or higher self so you can let go of lower, insecure, fear-based energies. Learn how to breathe deeply and properly, and connect to your body. Practices such as yoga, chi gong and meditation are based on the body-mind-life force connection and can quickly help you find balance.

Too many out-of-touch actors think it is enough to want a career. Time and time again, I have seen painfully self-conscious individuals make neurotic, defensive excuses about why their auditions didn't go well. There is no accountability, preparation, or understanding of the role nor is there any self-confidence. The lines are read flatly, head held down, and it seems like they can't wait for the audition to be over. There is nothing appealing about a self-imposed victimization, and it certainly won't get you a callback. Remember, at its core, arrogance is a lack of confidence, while confidence is a lack of arrogance.

Embrace and manage your humanity in all its imperfect beauty. Dare to explore the infinite possibilities of who you are. And learn to forgive yourself. Many of the best actors I know use attributes specific to themselves to great advantage. What may have been regarded as a flaw or weakness – height, weight or accent, for example, or other physical attributes - is transformed into a secret weapon. Also, having varied interests and a life outside of the industry is a major asset as this keeps you in touch with the reality of the world around you.

Stop forcing yourself to measure up to an impossible standard. That is highly detrimental and serves no purpose. We all experience states of depression at times, but we must find ways to overcome it, or we'll accomplish nothing. At it's most extreme, depression is narcissism turned inside out; try to avoid getting tangled in that net at all costs. One of the quickest and most fulfilling ways to get out of a deep funk is to help someone less fortunate than you are. Get out of your head and into a mode of giving. That puts you in an instant state of self-transformation!

Applying that spirit of service to auditioning and your place in the business is a gift you can give yourself. It becomes a soul-enhancing experience, a connection to what drew you to the industry in the first place. Identify the reasons why you are on the path you have chosen. Come up with two or three statements as to why you want to be a working actor, which is what you should aspire to be. As for stars, they burn out and fade.

I have two reasons why I chose to be a casting director and producer:

1) I want to help tell good stories.

2) I want to help actors get closer to their dreams.

It is really as simple as that. In the same way you must read the text to discover who and what your character is, you must listen to your heart to know who you really are.

AUDITION HOT TIP #19

Find an acting buddy. Form an alliance with a fellow actor; someone you won't be competing with for the same roles. Create a mutually beneficial support system. Commit to helping and supporting each other. Meet once a week to discuss the business and share professional insights, goals and progress. When preparing for auditions, run lines together and give constructive feedback. Like a gym buddy, you will become more motivated and less likely to procrastinate when there's someone else depending on you.

TO ACTORS WITH DISABILITIES

I was fortunate to have worked at a wonderful organization formerly known as the Non-Traditional Casting Project prior to becoming an independent casting director. My time working there opened my eyes to a community of artists, especially actors, each with a unique, individual perspective. When I launched Casting Solutions, it was only natural for me to include these actors as part of the talent pool. N.T.C.P. has recently changed its name to The Alliance for Inclusion in the Arts and is a wonderful resource for all. The organization can be reached at **www.inclusioninthearts.org.**

I recently attended a premiere of an original performance piece called "Inside/Out... voices from the disability community" commissioned by VSA arts, **www.vsarts.org**. VSA is an international organization that provides programs designed to increase access to the arts for people/artists with disabilities. A young actress named Blair Wing was one of the performers. In her piece, she says: "We may not be all the same, but we're not that much different either." She then goes on to use the term "mixed ability" instead of disability. When we spoke afterwards, she explained that the term came to her attention at grad school. While "disabled" has a negative connotation, "mixed abilities," whether emotional, physical, or mental is non-judgmental. Mixed abilities isn't positive or negative, just mixed, a term that is inclusive of all people. Thanks to Blair and her cast mates, I experienced a wonderful performance and learned a new tool for awareness that evening.

Most people, (unless they've had a personal experience with disability) are completely clueless; they cannot conceive of or appreciate the challenges faced each day. The entertainment industry, for the most part, reflects this insensitivity. So being strong and positive, even under the best of circumstances, can be daunting.

I have no disability-specific AUDITION HOT TIPS for you. All I can say (and this universally applies to ALL actors) is your acting skill has to be a priority as that is what will get you the job. The truth of the matter is that it is a production burden to accommodate PWD's. Consequently, a producer who is willing to pay for a ramp or extra insurance is the kind of producer who gets excited about working with the real deal: an actor hired for his or her artistic strengths. Please be encouraged that there are more and more enlightened members of the entertainment industry, who realize the importance and necessity of inclusion as an essential part of the casting process.

I urge you to cultivate your craft by any means necessary. Make them want to hire you because no one is quite like you. Understand that there aren't many roles to begin with, and bitterness and frustration only make the path more difficult. As a casting director, it is my responsibility to make producers and directors aware of the diverse options within the acting community. That said, train your heart out and prove them wrong.

ABOUT THE AUTHOR

Liz Ortiz-Mackes is a casting director, teacher and producer who has worked behind the scenes in the entertainment field since 1990. As the owner of Casting Solutions in New York City, Liz casts for film, theatre, television, commercials, industrials and digital media. An avid supporter of diversity in casting, she has been a SAG and Equity-franchised talent agent on both coasts, Director of Special Events at the Dramatists Guild and Director of Artists Files On-Line at the Non-Traditional Casting Project. Part of the special understanding and insight Liz brings to all that she does is based on her experience as a theatre director, directing plays in New York, Los Angeles, Boston and New Hampshire. Currently, Liz is on the faculty of the American Academy of Dramatic Arts, is a guest instructor at the New York Film Academy and conducts monthly workshops for the Screen Actors Guild Foundation. As a producer, she is working on several film and television projects in development. She lives in New York City with her husband and two sons.

For more information, or to book an Iconic Specificity™ Workshop with Liz, email: **castsolutions@aol.com**

RESOURCES

Call Sheet by Back Stage (formerly known as "The Ross Reports")

How to be a Working Actor   by Mari Lyn Henry and Lynne Rogers

Ask an Agent   by Margaret Emory

Talking Funny for Money   by Pamela Lewis

Happy for No Reason   by Marci Shimoff

Flowdreaming   by Summer McStravick

www.backstage.com

www.actorsaccess.com

www.theatricalindex.com

www.playbill.com

www.everythingactingpodcast.com

www.sabellamills.com
(Top Voice Teacher, Broadway Star, David Sabella-Mills)

www.cahillconnolly.com
(My Casting Associate is an amazing Headshot Photographer)

www.castingsolutions.tv
(MY WEBSITE!)

NOTES

NOTES

Made in the USA
Lexington, KY
29 June 2011